My
Baby Record
Album

Bluestreak
BOOKS

Illustrated by Ximena Jeria
Written by Elizabeth Golding
Designed by Anton Poitier

Published in North America by Bluestreak Books
An Imprint of Weldon Owen
Weldon Owen is a Division of Bonnier Publishing USA
1045 Sansome Street, Suite 100, San Francisco, CA 94111
www.WeldonOwen.com

Library of Congress Cataloging in Publication Data is available.

ISBN: 978-1-68188-288-8

This album was created by

with a bit of
help from:

begun this day

Before birth

Baby's due date _____

Ultrasound scan dates _____

Where birth is planned _____

Our thoughts:

We think you will look like

_____

_____

_____

Baby names

Mom's favorite names for a girl

....

....

Dad's favorite names for a girl

....

....

Mom's favorite names for a boy

....

....

Dad's favorite names for a boy

....

....

The name we chose and why

....

....

....

....

....

About your arrival

Birth date ....

Time ....

Place ....

Weight ....

Length ....

Eye color ....

Hair color ....

Midwife's name ....

Doctor's name ....

Who was at the birth ....

The weather that day ....

When we took you home ....

Hospital tag

Coming home

Coming home date ....

Baby was wearing ....

First visitors ....

Mommy slept for ....

Breast fed or bottle fed ....

My coming home photo taken by

....

About you

On the day you were born

Our favorite song

Famous people in the news that day

Milk cost

Bread cost

A postage stamp cost

The good news

We sent the good news to our family and friends:

Family tree

Mommy's family

Grandma ....

Grandpa ....

Aunts ....

....

....

Uncles ....

....

....

Daddy's family

Grandma ....

Grandpa ....

Aunts ....

....

....

Uncles ....

....

....

Getting used to baby

Baby's first diaper was changed by

Who gets up most at night

What happens at bath time

What happens at bedtime

First night you slept through

Progress

Length / height	Weight
Birth	
1 month	
2 months	
3 months	
4 months	
5 months	
6 months	
7 months	
8 months	
9 months	
10 months	
11 months	
12 months	

Birth presents

Our family and friends brought these gifts for you

Little firsts

First sat up ....

First shuffle ....

First crawled ....

First stood up ....

Took first steps with some help ....

Took first steps unaided ....

First steps

My first steps were on this day:

_____

location and who was there:

_____

_____

My first steps photo taken by

_____

First lock of hair

My first lock of hair was
put in this envelope on:

First hand print

We made a hand print on this day ....

helped me make my hand print

Birth signs

Aries
March 21 - April 19

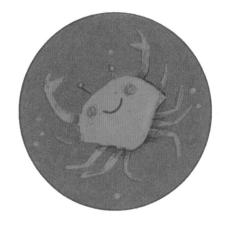

Cancer
June 21 - July 22

Taurus
April 20 - May 20

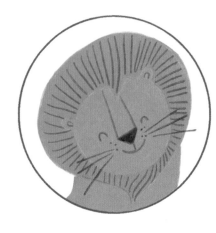

Leo
July 23 - August 22

Gemini
May 21 - June 20

Virgo
August 23 - September 22

Baby's birth sign _____

Libra
September 23 - October 22

Capricorn
December 22 - January 19

Scorpio
October 23 - November 21

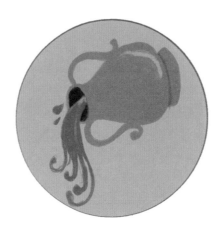

Aquarius
January 20 - February 18

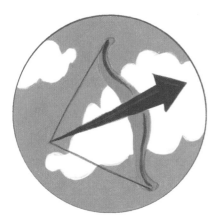

Sagittarius
November 22 - December 21

Pisces
February 19 - March 20

First Christmas

My first Santa wishes:

My favorite Christmas things:

My first Christmas photo:

My first Christmas photo taken by:

....

Visitors for baby's first Christmas

First Easter

We went on an Easter outing to

We had an Easter egg hunt

Who came to visit

Your favorite Easter gift

Your best friends are

Some things to remember

....

_____

_____

....

My first Easter photo taken by

....

First birthday

My best first birthday photo
was taken by:

....

At:

....

....

First birthday party

My first birthday party
guests were:

....

....

....

....

....

....

Baby's firsts

First slept through ....

Lifted head ....

Rolled over ....

First smile ....

First laugh ....

Chews toys ....

First tooth ....

Sits up ....

Eats solids ....

Drinks from a sippy cup ....

Played peek-a-boo ....

First clapped ....

Sat in a high chair ....

Played with fingers ....

Played with toes ....

Bath time fun

My bath time photo taken by

First bath

Who bathes baby

My bath time favorites

Bedtime

Our special time is

First night in a crib

First night baby sleeps through

Who reads bedtime story

Favorite story

First trip out

My first trip out photo taken by

We went to

What we did

Best part of the day

Baby's first words

Baby's first words were

....

....

....

....

Baby first said 'Mommy' on

....

Baby first said 'Daddy' on

....

First holiday

We went to

....

Favorite moments

....

....

....

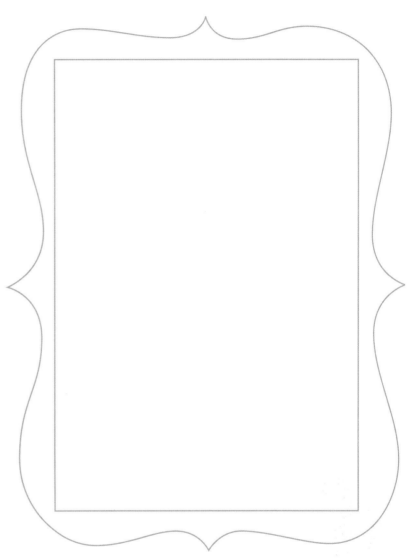

My first holiday photo taken by

....

Baby's favorites

Food ....

Drink ....

Toy ....

Game ....

Activity ....

Animal ....

Song ....

Story ....

Place ....

TV ....

Film ....

....

....

....

Baby's little
friends

My friends in this photo

....

....

....

Baby's health

Health visitor

Doctor

Dentist

Immunization details

Type	Date

Our wishes for baby

This is what Mommy thinks
baby will do as a grown up:

_____
_____
_____
_____
_____

This is what Daddy thinks
baby will do as a grown up:

_____
_____
_____
_____
_____

This is what our friends think
baby will do as a grown up:

_____
_____
_____

Hush Little Baby

Hush, little baby, don't say a word,
Mama's gonna buy you a mockingbird.

And if that mockingbird don't sing,
Mama's gonna buy you a diamond ring.

And if that diamond ring turns brass,
Mama's gonna buy you a looking glass.

And if that looking glass is broke,
Mama's gonna buy you a billy goat,

And if that billy goat won't pull,
Mama's gonna buy you a cart and a bull.

And if that cart and bull turn over,
Mama's gonna buy you a dog named Rover.

And if that dog named Rover won't bark,
Mama's gonna buy you a horse and a cart.

And if that horse and cart fall down,
You'll still be the sweetest little baby in town.

So hush little baby, don't you cry.
Daddy loves you and so do I.

Twinkle, twinkle, little star

Twinkle, twinkle, little star,
How I wonder what you are!
Up above the world so high,
Like a diamond in the sky.

When the blazing sun is gone,
When he nothing shines upon,
Then you show your little light,
Twinkle, twinkle, through the night.

Then the traveler in the dark
Thanks you for your tiny spark;
He could not see where to go,
If you did not twinkle so.

In the dark blue sky you keep,
And often through my curtains peep,
For you never shut your eye
Till the sun is in the sky.

As your bright and tiny spark
Lights the traveler in the dark,
Though I know not what you are,
Twinkle, twinkle, little star.

Rock a bye baby

Rock a bye baby, in the tree top
When the wind blows, the cradle will rock
When the bough breaks, the cradle will fall
And down will come baby, cradle and all

Hickory dickory dock

Hickory, dickory, dock.
The mouse ran up the clock.
The clock struck one,
The mouse ran down,
Hickory, dickory, dock.

Bye, baby Bunting

Bye, baby Bunting,
Daddy's gone a-hunting,
Gone to get a rabbit skin
To wrap the baby Bunting in.

Brahm's lullaby

Lullaby and goodnight,
With roses bedight,
With lilies o'er spread
Is baby's wee bed.
Lay thee down now and rest,
May thy slumber be blessed.

Lullaby and goodnight,
Thy mother's delight,
Bright angels beside
My darling abide.
They will guard thee at rest,
Thou shalt wake on my breast.

Little Blessings

Our special blessing was

_____

On this day

_____

With whom

_____

Special celebrations

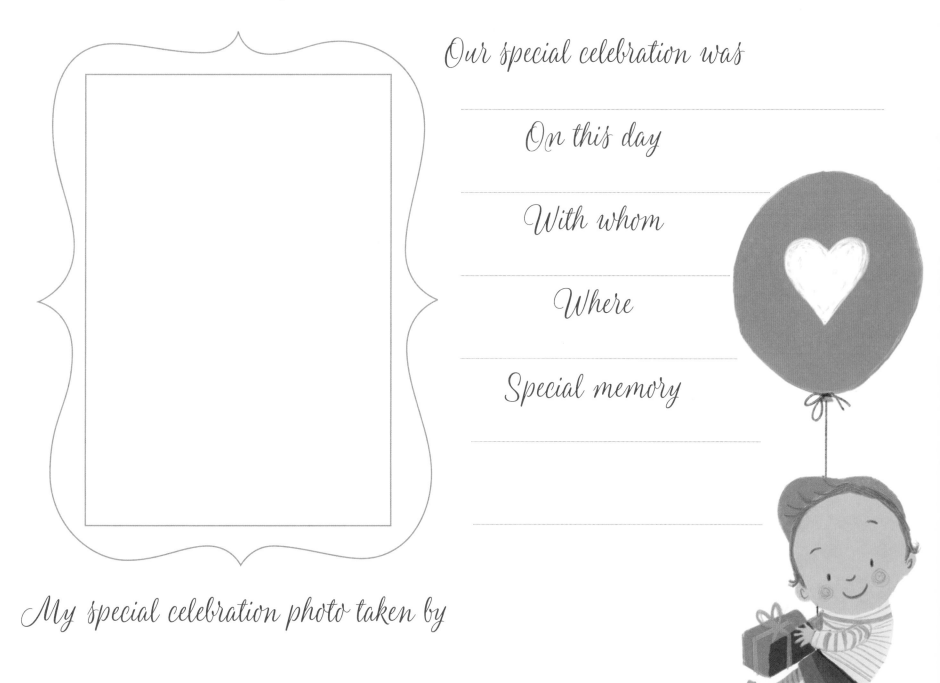

Our special celebration was

On this day

With whom

Where

Special memory

My special celebration photo taken by

2nd birthday

My 2nd birthday party was

_____

Special memory

_____

With whom

_____

_____

My 2nd birthday photo taken by

2nd birthday memories

2nd Christmas

My Santa wishes

My favorite Christmas things

What we did at Christmas

Christmas memories

My 2nd Christmas photo taken by

3rd birthday

My 3rd birthday party was

....

Special memory

....

With whom

....

....

My 3rd birthday photo taken by
....

3rd birthday memories

3rd Christmas

My Santa wishes:

_____

_____

_____

My favorite Christmas things:

_____

_____

_____

Christmas memories

_____

_____

_____

_____

_____

_____

My third Christmas photos:

My 3rd Christmas photo taken by

My 3rd Christmas photo taken by

First day at kindergarten or nursery

Name of kindergarten or nursery ....

First day ....

Best friend ....

First day memories

....

....

....

....

....

....

....

My kindergarten picture

Special memories

4th birthday

My 4th birthday party was

Special memory

With whom

First rode a bicycle

Riding my bike photo taken by

First rode a bicycle

Where

With whom

4th Christmas

My Santa wishes:

....

....

....

My favorite Christmas things:

....

....

....

Christmas memories

....

....

....

....

....

....

My 4th Christmas photos:

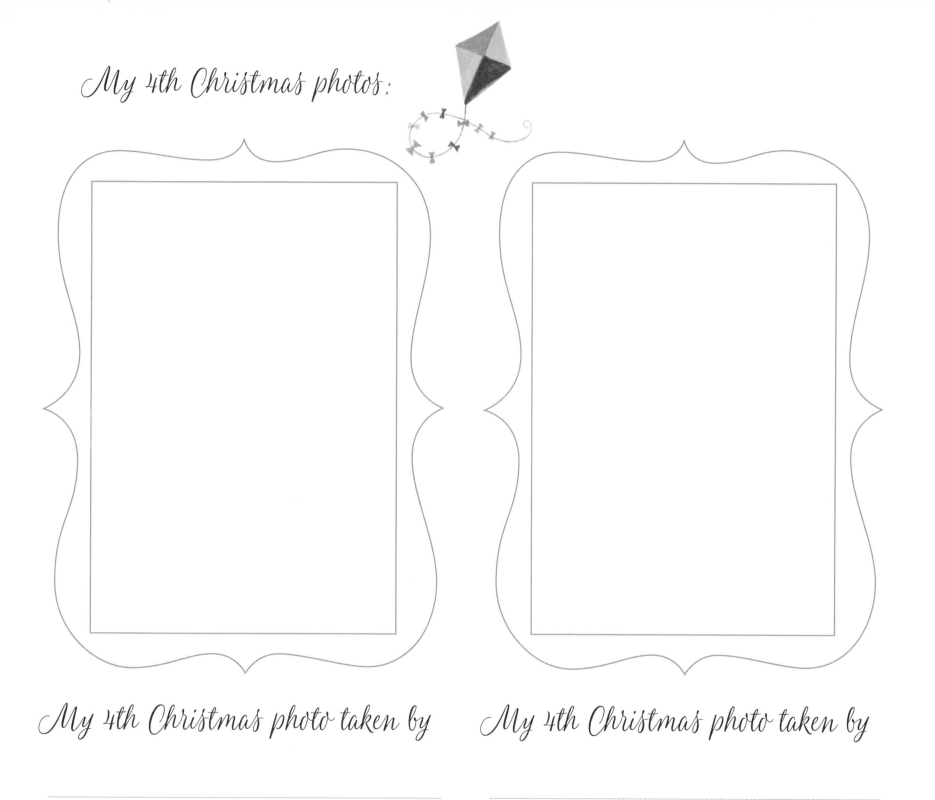

My 4th Christmas photo taken by

My 4th Christmas photo taken by

5th birthday

My 5th birthday party was

_____

Special memory

_____

With whom

_____

_____

My 5th birthday photo taken by

5th birthday memories

5th Christmas

Christmas wishes:

....

....

....

Christmas memories

....

....

....

....

My 5th Christmas photo taken by

....

First day at school

Name of elementary school ....

First day at elementary school ....

Best friend at school ....

First day memories

My best friends at 5

These are my friends: